# TECHNICAL SKILLS

## COMPILED AND EDITED BY JANE MAGRATH

## CONTENTS

**A complete piano method based on the classics**

(All loosely correlated with *Alfred's Basic Piano Library*—with corresponding levels)

*Masterwork Classics* Levels 1–6

*Practice and Performance* Levels 1–6

*Technical Skills* Levels 1–6

Second Edition

Copyright © MCMXCIX by Alfred Publishing Co., Inc.

All rights reserved. Printed in USA.

Cover art: Planet Art

PhotoDisc

## PURPOSE

These exercises will help students develop fluent fingers and flexibility in moving about the keyboard. The degree of flexibility developed in the warm-ups exceeds that demanded in the repertoire at this point in order to keep the students' technique ahead of the demands of the music.

## MAY BE LEARNED BY ROTE

It is suggested that these warm-ups be presented by rote. They are all based on easy-to-learn patterns that the student should be able to remember. However, several of these pieces enhance the sound by featuring rhythmic values that some students may not have studied and for which special attention may be needed. Also, since the warm-ups encourage the student to utilize the entire keyboard, their study by rote may make them easier to play. Average students at this book's level of difficulty also will be able to read the warm-ups with minimal explanation concerning rhythm and leger lines.

## HOW TO PRACTICE

Each warm-up should be played over an extended period of time, not just for one or two weeks. The goal is to develop fluency and flexibility. Students should learn to play these exercises with dynamic inflection and nuance, with the right hand voiced above the left hand and alternately with the left hand voiced above the right hand, matching tones in sequence and with evenness of technique. These practices may be extended to such exercises as playing the right hand staccato while the left hand is legato, and so on. The goals can provide guidance for teacher and student in working out the examples. Teachers are encouraged to make modifications in the exercises, either temporarily or permanently. For instance, an example with dotted rhythms might be played for several weeks with even rhythms before dotted rhythms are used.

## HOW MANY EXERCISES AT ONCE?

A student should be playing two or three (perhaps even four) of the warm-ups in different stages as part of daily practice. The student should learn to listen for evenness in technique, phrasing and nuance.

## WHAT IF...

*An exercise is too hard for a student at first?* Have the student practice only one or two repetitions of the pattern until that is mastered. Then assign more of the pattern to be played. The *Crawling* versions of the warm-ups make them easy to assign in this way.

*The student cannot play in a steady tempo?* The student should play the example much slower with a steady beat and strong pulse. All of the warm-ups should sound like mini-pieces and should display musical inflection and shaping. Students should count all examples carefully.

*The student has been introduced to several of the five-finger patterns?* He/she should transpose the examples to the major (or minor) five-finger patterns. In this first book, *Crawling* versions of the exercises simply progress upward using the white keys only. If possible, it is preferable for the student to play the examples in major five-finger positions. Later books will ask that the patterns be played in the major and minor finger positions.

Warm-Up No. 1
# Creeping Along

*Continue upward on white keys until…*

Warm-Up No. 2

# Free at Last

### Warm-Up No. 2a  (Crawling Version)

*Continue upward on white keys until…*

Warm-Up No. 3
# Working Diligently

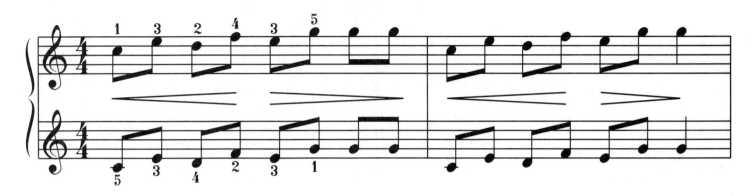

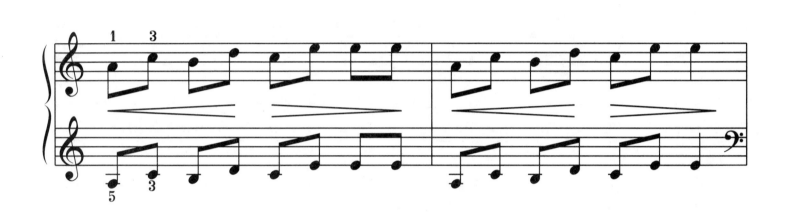

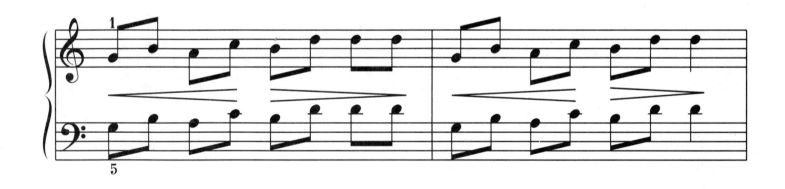

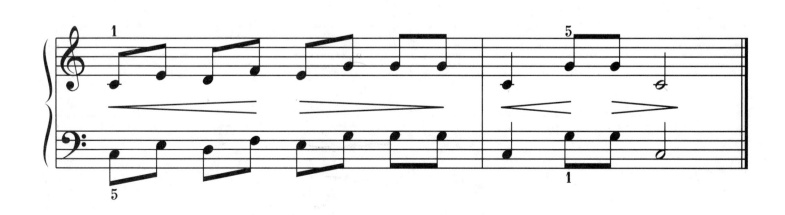

# Hot-Air Balloons

## Warm-Up No. 4a  (Crawling Version)

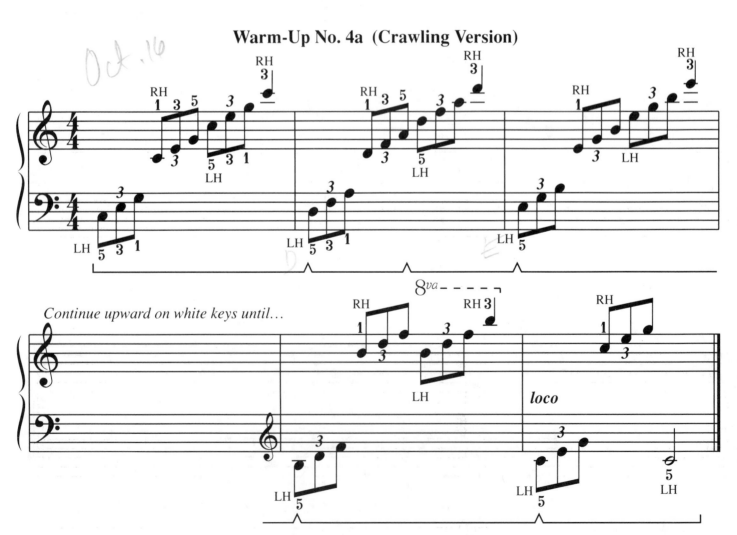

*Continue upward on white keys until…*

## Warm-Up No. 5
# Awesome Mountains

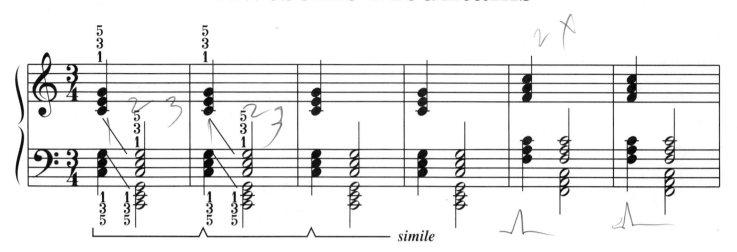

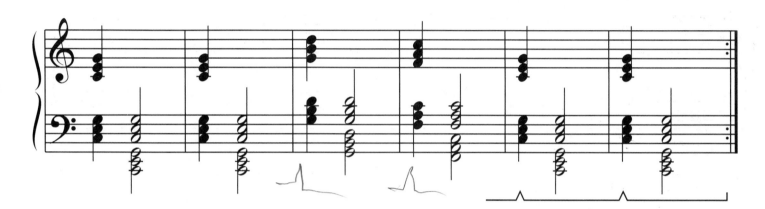

## Warm-Up No. 5a  (Crawling Version)

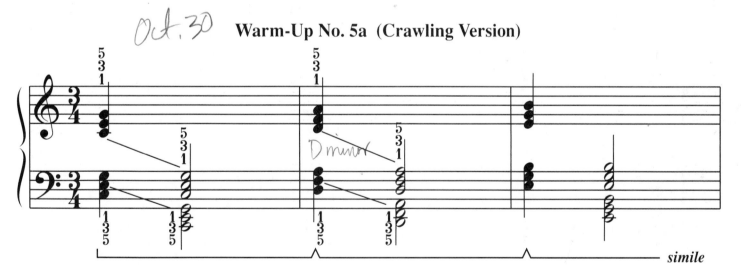

*Continue upward on white keys until…*

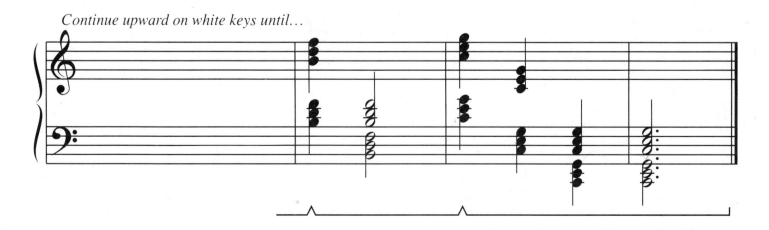

*Nov*

## Warm-Up No. 6
# Jazzy Fingers

*Continue upward on white keys until:*

Warm-Up No. 7

# Going Round 'n' Round

Warm-Up No. 8

# Mr. Alberti

*Continue based on No. 7.*

## Warm-Up No. 9
# Chord March

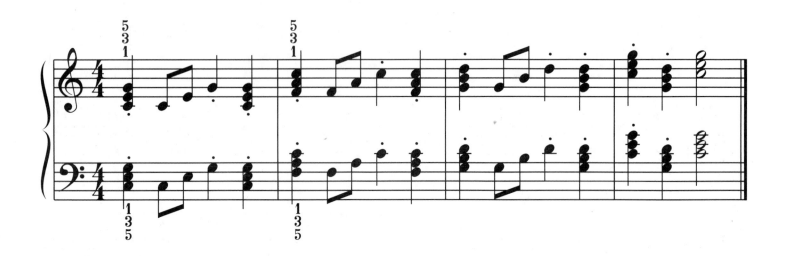

**Warm-Up No. 9a  (Crawling Version)**

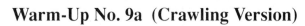

*Continue upward on white keys until…*

**Warm-Up No. 10**
# Attending a Wedding

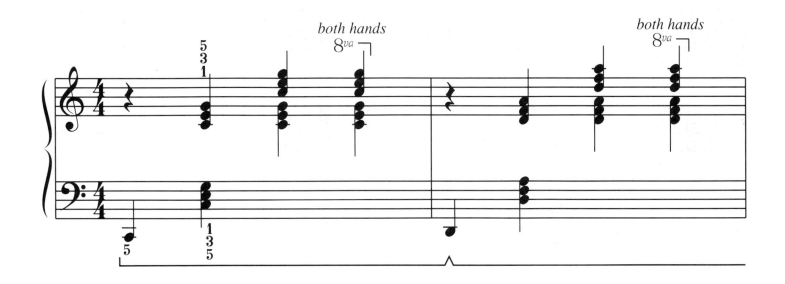

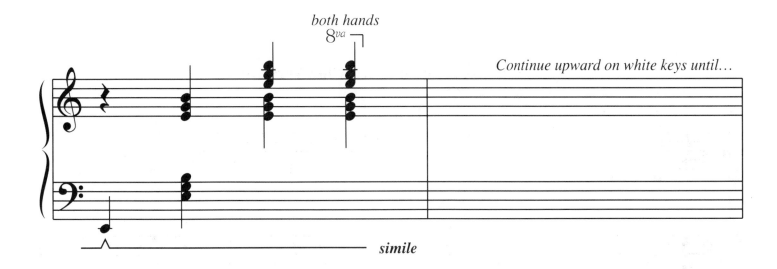

*Continue upward on white keys until…*

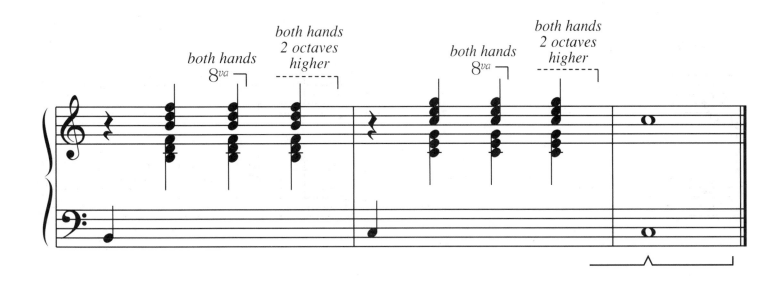

# ETUDES

## HOW TO PRACTICE

The études are taken from standard collections of études from past centuries. They are included to help the student develop fluency and facility for playing the standard literature as well as reading skills. Students should practice the études carefully to develop properly choreographed hand movements and proficient technique. If possible, the students should practice transposing some of these études to other keys. All examples should be played with a sense of phrasing and nuance, and students should be encouraged to watch their hands for proper movements and motions.

## TITLES

Suggested titles have been provided by the editor and compiler to enhance the student's imagery when working on these selections. The titles often are programmatic and attempt to suggest a mood or character for the music.

## KEY CENTERS

Several études have been transposed to other keys since virtually all teaching études were originally written in the key of C major. These transpositions allow for a variety of sound and relieve the monotony of a single key. Those études transposed from C to the keys used in this edition are: Berens's *Etude, Op. 70, No. 4*, Köhler's *Etude, Op. 190, No. 15*, Czerny's *Etude, Op. 823, No. 6*, Berens's *Etude, Op. 70, No. 8* and Czerny's *Etude, Op. 823, No. 22*.

# Etude
### (Waltzing Tennis Shoes)

Hermann Berens (1826–1880)
Op. 70, No. 4

# Etude
### (Carousel)

Louis Köhler (1820–1886)
Op. 190, No. 8

# Etude
### (Tumbling Down)

Louis Köhler (1820–1886)
Op. 190, No. 13

# Etude
### (The French Balloon)

Louis Köhler (1820–1886)
Op. 190, No. 15

# Etude

### (Say it Again!)

Carl Czerny (1791–1857)
Op. 823, No. 6

# Etude
## (Walking on Tiptoe)

Carl Czerny (1791–1857)
Op. 823, No. 9

# Etude
## (Promenade)

Hermann Berens (1826–1880)
Op. 70, No. 8

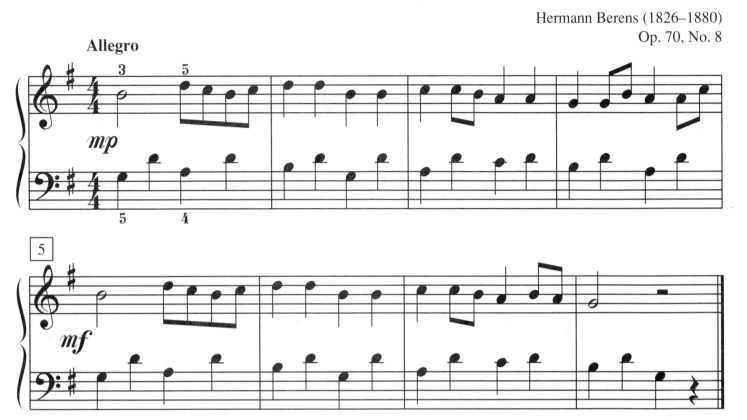

# Song

Cornelius Gurlitt (1820–1901)
from *A First Book*

# Etude
## (A Conversation)

Cornelius Gurlitt (1820–1901)
Op. 117, No. 9

# Etude

## (Fanfare)

Carl Czerny (1791–1857)
Op. 823, No. 11

# Two Are Playing

Cornelius Gurlitt (1820–1901)
from *A First Book*

# Etude
### (Fox Hunt)

Carl Czerny (1791–1857)
Op. 823, No. 22

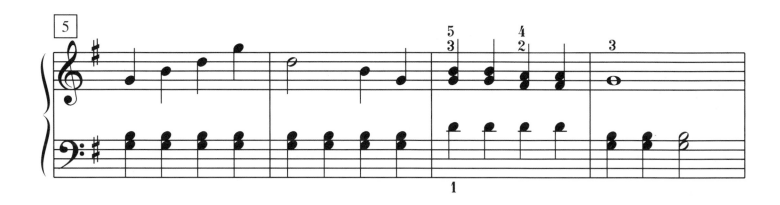

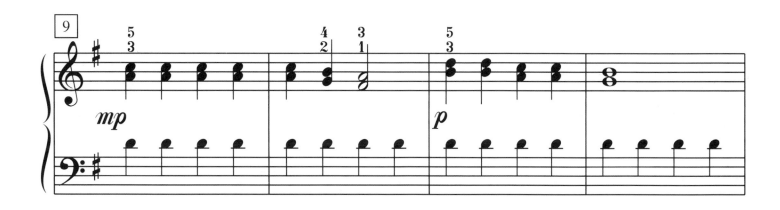

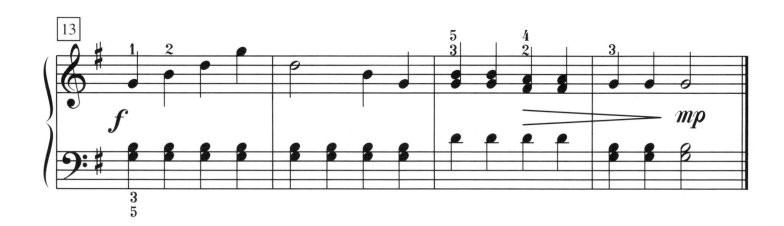

# Etude

## (Whitewater Rafting)

Carl Czerny (1791–1857)
Op. 777, No. 3

# Etude

## (Hymn)

Ludwig Schytte (1848–1909)
Op. 108, No. 3

# TO THE TEACHER

### ESTABLISH GOALS

Goals should be established for the student's practice of an exercise over a period of weeks. For instance, focus one week on evenness and facility, the next week include nuance and matching tones, then work to voice the right hand louder then the left hand, etc. These same kinds of goals should be established for the études. It is important that the student know not only to practice an activity, but *how* to practice that activity and what to look and listen for while practicing.

### ROTE TEACHING OF EXERCISES

Students may find it easier, and teachers more satisfying, if the exercises are presented initially by rote, and then read from the score. All exercises are highly patterned so that the student can learn them quickly, and then watch the hands for proper movements, and so on. All exercises may be used successfully whether read from the book or played by rote. Help students see the patterns in the exercises so that they can be memorized sooner and remembered longer.

### REMEMBER TO ENJOY PLAYING THE TECHNICAL AND MUSICAL DRILLS

Play the warm-ups and études so that they are musical and make musical sense. Encourage the student to compose additional warm-ups based on the patterns presented and to create additional titles for the études and the warm-ups. Inspire creativity and encourage the student to listen to the music to discover what it may express. Enjoy the total music making process!

### ACKNOWLEDGMENTS

Heartfelt appreciation for their help in preparing this volume is expressed to Morty and Iris Manus and Patrick Wilson. The author also gratefully acknowledges the assistance of Nancy Neal, Tom Pearsall and Michelle Robison.